I Am Very David

David Lawrence

Contents

My Wife is my Wife is my Wife

I Grab onto all the Forms of Mental Illness and Finger them

Narcissism

I am Narcissus. I fall in love with my own reflection and drown in the love of myself, my image, my whomever I am in a pond.

You find me loathsome. I find me in a forest making love to myself. Masturbation is a form of self-cohabitation. I am attracted to my attraction.

I am the king of self-congratulation. Grandiosity is the lack of self-confidence boiled in a pot of attempted self-love.

I don't fit in with the mundane. I am a personality disorder. I am dizzy in a pool of self-congratulation.

You say that I don't give a damn about you. How could I? I am too busy admiring myself. It's not that I am grandiose. It's that I am all that exists.

I am not arrogant. I do not believe in comparisons. No one exists beyond myself. Arrogance involves this and that and I am above weighing the evidence. I am just this and that, alone, and self-being.

I am the king of everyone else's castles. I am special. Without me the country would not exist. When I went to England in my teens I stood next to a guard and pretended that I was an historical warrior. I jousted when I jested about my greatness.

We are the Knights of the Roundtable. We drink to ourselves. We kiss our own metal gloves. We praise ourselves. We lift our lances and swords and fight off insults.

My admiration for myself is not excessive. I am excessive. I am grandiose. You are jealous. I am the reason for castles.

I fall in love with my reflection. I am my reflection. I see myself looking back at whomever I am from my excessive pool.

Obama was the President of narcissism. I am the king of royal self-love. My grandeur is in my bones. I know it. He didn't. I enjoy the self-discovery of drowning.

I am proud of my genetic love of my reflection.

Disorder

My moods are out of order. They are boots with broken heels tripping on the road to self-discovery. But there are no revelations because there is no center at the heart of chaotic being.

I do not exist. I am merely a result of chemistry. I feel what I feel not because of circumstance but because the insides of my body fluctuate like mixed vials.

I am a potion. I am an ocean of chemicals that dictate what I do and say. Hey, hey, hey I am a product of my body.

Lithium's chemistry calms me. It turns my violence down with a few little pills. Without it I am scrabble tiles falling from the sky.

When I get depressed I can't give the sadness a rest. I am the result of the initial presumption. I don't cry. Sadness is its own wetness.

When I am happy and flying over the town like Mary Poppins I know what it is to be a happy piece of God. I am omnipotent and all powerful. Mania whips me about like a weathervane in a tornado.

I want to kiss myself. Call it a masturbatory smooch. I get closer to myself than to other people. I am so happy to meet me. I am so happy to be me. I am the disorder of inflation in a rising balloon.

Am I a mood disorder? What do I care? Greatness is its own interpretation and I am happy to meet me. I single myself out at the party. I am dancing with my shadow.

Paranoia

Paranoia is a cheap disease where the victim imagines that he is being hit on the head with bags of pennies and becomes lumpy in his suspicion. Help me. Help you. The cries are panic in a cake, frosting on unhappiness, warts on toads.

I am not paranoid. You are paranoid looking at me accusing me of something wrong.

I am right. I am a turn in a garden where I end up in bundles of colorful flowers. I am not a weedy paranoid. I don't think anyone is after me. I am before me. I am grandeur walking down a carpet in Oz. Or perhaps I am walking in Odd.

I am not deluded by grandeur. At least not the grandeur of persecution. I am not afraid of you or you or you. You can't hurt me because you can't hurt God. I am peeking out of the curtains of religion. But I am a powerless God.

I can't hurt anyone. I do not wipe humanity from the face of the earth every hundred or so years. I am not a napkin on the lips of humanity. I am not the mean recipient of all of our prayers.

I am just the magnificence of magnificence. I am as beautiful as I am sad and forlorn. I am not paranoid. I am above that.

I am not sick. I am not schizophrenic. I am a beautiful nude Greek marble statue at the Metropolitan Museum of Art. I am the cloud that rains on the earthbound cloud and washes my eyes clear with vision.

What I like about being almost crazy is that I fly above the pedestrian sidewalks where the sane lack imagination.

Schizophrenia

I walked into a wall where "schizophrenia" was written in red paint.
It dripped onto my face.
I became an Indian in war paint fighting
against myself.
Did I become schizophrenic?
I don't know.
I don't think I climbed up to the last rung of craziness.
My thoughts attacked my emotions and my behavior became erratic.
That was not erotic.
I became soft and depressed.
My actions elbowed my romantic delusions and my life sentence
became fragmented.
I became a contradiction.
But I was not as mad as a broken wall in a hail storm in the suburbs.
I was not nuts.
I was the squirrel who ate the nuts.
I still knew who I was in a vague foreign sort of way and I found myself
in fifty-two cards where the dealer is wearing black gloves and losing.
I was somewhere in between schizophrenia and tripping along
someone else's route in borrowed madness.

Piss Phobia

I am piss shy or phobic about pissing in public bathrooms whether
in stalls or at urinals because it is all the same,
all samples of shame,
an admission that I have a dick,
thick,
maybe but it is its awkward essence that turns me red
like when I blushed when twenty feds raided my Wall Street office.
Why me?
I suppose I was easy and not dangerous.
I wasn't afraid of being raided.
I wanted to stand up to misplaced adversity.
But to piss in public is an embarrassing thing,
a disgusting pass time,
and I don't like to take my dick out even if I am hidden by a stall.
Sometimes I have to go so bad that I close the door behind me
and sit on the toilet like a woman
so imaginary people can't see my dick when I put it between my
legs and piss.
Of course I have to jiggle it around somewhat.
Sometimes I pour some water from a bottle on it so that it gets
used to wetness and is encouraged to squirt.
You could say I'm not a real pisser.
I try.
After all if it backs up too much into my kidneys or whatever
biological part hurts.
I only pissed in my pants once.
It was in kindergarten.
The students were standing at our desks before we were sent home.
I couldn't hold it any longer.

I pissed on the floor.
I don't remember if anyone saw it.
I should but I don't.
When I got home my thigh developed a rash.
I don't know if my piss phobia has anything to do with that
kindergarten accident.
Life is a circle.

Piss is to be contained.
Sometimes it has its own will power like a warrior.
When I sit on the toilet I wave my penis round and around,
blush as I must,
like I am communicating with the God of urine and climbing
my own anatomical stairway (Eric Clapton) to heaven.

Crazy

You are mentally ill or so they say. Hey, hey, hey so am I.
How now brown cow?
How am I crazy when I think that I am a rapture of sanity?
What's the difference?
I don't know.
I was 4-F from Vietnam for being insane.
I got disability from social security when I was forty-six.
The MTA charges me half price because I am half bizarre.
What's the difference?
My sanity or insanity is a small pittance compared
to all that I know.
I know not.
I know a lot.
Who knows?
I never killed myself.
I am still here contemplating what I am and am not.
I know so little that I know a bunch about the little in the mirror
and madness in the glass.
There is something exciting about being insane and
madness is a flower that I pluck and put in my button hole
to attract pretty women to prettiness.
I am disappointed that I was never in a mental institution.
I would have liked to prove my crazy pedigree.
But I am left wandering in the grassy fields of myself where
no labels bring me down.
Maybe my sanity is a reverse posture of the shoulders of my madness.
Say hello. Say goodbye. Say that nothing matters when your
mood is high.

Yeah, OCD Again

Yeah, I know I've told you before about my OCD but I can't get my obsessions out of my head when they are manifest here and there and everywhere and nowhere. I don't care. My intrusive thoughts come and go like works by Michelangelo, like my deluded grand impressions of my own poems.

Call me bipolar. I don't care. I am very David who is like a phat beat in a rap song. I did three rap albums. "Renegade Jew" was almost famous. I had no rhythm. I was all about the lyrics. I was a genius who walked on out-of-tune stumps.

I am not compulsive. I don't believe in action. I torture myself in a quiet world of jagged thoughts. There is no outside world. I am snow shoveled into an alley. I look into myself and fish for my sadness at the bottom of the pond.

The thing I like about boxing is getting punched in the face. When I get a facial bruise I feel close to myself. I am tight. I am in love with me.

I like jail too. I don't like freedom. It is too restrictive for wide open generalities and I would rather be closed in with my obsessions.

I am looking forward to death. I want to cuddle into myself and find identity in disintegration. I hope my poems live after me. If they don't, it doesn't matter because I lived with them in my pockets like spare change for decades of self-love.

Did I have a good time on earth? *Come se, come ca.* Suicide was a small option. I wanted to be part of the earth, the grass, the trees, the people, the globe, everything that I hated and loved and couldn't make my mind up about.

It is not easy to be David. In fact it is very, very. But I feel a little more worthy and grand than being you. No offense. Don't hit me. Oh, go ahead and punch me in the face.

Mescaline and Max's

Hallucinations scare me because I can't run on a tread mill that keeps shaking and turning. I need steadiness in my Bosco.

When I was young I drank chocolate milk like Will Smith in "Men in Black." It steadied me like I sucked on the nipple of the cow of the universe.

When I was twenty-one my friend, Ken. slipped some mescaline in my wine at Max's Kansas City. I hallucinated like a nervous break-down. My consciousness divided into pieces of visual delusion. I saw fists coming out of the walls and punching me in the eye.

I panicked. I wanted to cry but I had forgotten how to tear up. I shook like a skinny tree in a windstorm.

I heard voices but I couldn't understand what they were saying. I was talking to myself while I didn't understand the voices. I was saying, "You really fucked yourself up."

My friend Ken drove me back to his parents' house in Great Neck. We sat and talked about nothing for five hours.

The whole time I was worried that my mind would fracture into pieces and I would break down into a pile of thoughts and fears on the floor.

I was not insane. I was drugged. I saw that there was no fun in mescaline or a gun. I didn't want to die but my peacefulness had fractured. I was afraid of what I had become.

I wanted to wait out the drug and hug my own equanimity. I would never take mescaline again. I didn't. I was good at giving up bad habits. I know how to turn away. I didn't need the ten steps program. Just one firm step like Hans Solo's leap of faith.

Delusions

There are times when I hallucinate, lactate (no, not me), over-rate my intelligence. Oh, I don't know what I mean.

A delusion is a delusion is a delusion. It is a belief in what isn't really there and an inference instead of a conviction.

I am deluded. I am grand. I am God but not Christ because why should I be the Son when I could be the dad. And I don't like nails in my palms. I want to punish pain but not be punished by it.

I am not stupid. I don't hallucinate. I know what is real. I don't mistake what is for what isn't and what isn't for what it is.

Sometimes I see faces popping out of walls. Oh, that was on mescaline in 1969.

The other day I saw a man walking down the street without a head. Is that an hallucination or my cataracts?

I am competitive. I want to be the craziest man in the world. I want to be so crazy that I am God. I am. I taste good like a yam. I lick my hand like a peasant kissing the Pope's ring.

Pope Francis is a bad man. Why? I don't remember. My thoughts invade me from outer space. I am heaven's dunce.

The Therapy of Jail

The thing I love about jail is that it reminds me of a session with
the psychiatrist.
I am all alone regardless of the other prisoners.
I am lost in myself
like Hansel and Gretel in the woods.
I am close to the other thugs but only at a distance.
I don't get close
but I wander around them like a boat around its anchor.
All the white elites in their atheist covens moan about the mis-
treatment of prisoners.
They don't cry about the dead victims in their trail.
The mistreatment of felons is not by the guards but the other
grungy cons.
I'd rather room with the correction officers than the criminals.
Nothing matters.
I was brave.
I had been a professional fighter and the criminals knew my rap songs.
I would have been happy to kill someone.
I never outgrew my anger from when I was fifteen.
I don't care.
Beware, I am unpredictable in a structured prison world.

Neurotic

I am insulted that you think that I am only neurotic like bland
bread crumbs when I am convinced that I am the tang of jam.

I am the order of disorder,
the consistency of misplaced thoughts
and the anxiety of hurt
where pain is an afterthought
and after becomes present.

I am obsessional and can't shake certain repetitive thoughts like
poking out my eyes or raping a lamppost to see the light
of aggression.

I don't do compulsive acts because I am obsessive
and action means nothing to me.
Silence is a loud noise
in retreat.

I am not a hypochondriac about diseases because I don't care if I
live or die.
I am always sick.
When I cough I imagine I have tuberculosis?
That might be fun.
I am Hans Castorp.
I always wanted to live in Thomas Mann's "Magic Mountain."

Anxiety in a Fish Tank

Do I have a mood disorder or are my disorders different types of moods?
I am neither this nor that but my beats are phat in a rap sort of way.
Am I schizophrenic or do my moods resemble
the madness they are not when
they are disappearing from reasonable postures?
I am anxiety in a fish tank,
a display of a piece of the aggravated ocean.
I panic or I don't panic.
I eat fear like a waffle and calm down in maple syrup.
When I went to jail I laughed.
I am not afraid of what other people fear because I know that
peace lies beneath Kurtz's horror.
The jungle that doesn't exist is the precursor to death.
Phobias are weaknesses that cowards feel like broken bones.
I am obsessive compulsive.
I am pushed along like a snowbank by a snowplow.
There are disorders in my chemistry and I find myself alive in a
test tube truth.
The euphoria of my depression is the compulsive nature of my
governance.
In the heart of darkness there is the light of resolution.

Jailed Brain

The thing I love about jail is that it reminds me of a session with
the psychiatrist.
I am all alone regardless of the other prisoners.
I am lost in myself
like Hansel and Gretel in the woods.
I am close to the other thugs but only at a distance.
I don't get close
but I wander around them like a boat around its anchor.
I laugh at my buddies who complain about the food.
I ate at Four-star restaurants and I still tolerate this mulch.
Am I strange?
Am I insane?
Be a man not a malcontent.
Be me if you want to go in the opposite direction to the wind and
still beat up in the direction the gusts are blowing from.
I am not locked-in in jail.
I am wandering the wide spaces of my tightening mind.
My brain is jailed from the outside world and I find freedom in my
closure.
White liberals all cry for the blacks who are jailed.
I don't see them crying for me.
I cry for them because they are so clichéd in their simplistic love
of the poor.
Fuck the sympathetic elite.
I am looking for my punishment behind bars in closed in places.

Intrusive

I have had so many intrusive thoughts in my life that I intrude,
am rude, fool myself with self-infliction,
dereliction,
and think that I am going to poke my eyes out,
rape a little girl,
kick a cane or a walker out from under an old lady's hands.
These thoughts mean nothing to me except to make me fearful
of my own loss of control.
Why do I do it?
To hurt myself because I feel that I should be punished for
whatever
I did or didn't when I was young.
Did my mother hate me?
I don't think so.
But I sense her rejection and go out naked in the cold to feel
the icy fingers of regret when I can't find a shawl to cover me.
Do my negative thoughts intrude my peace or negate my positive
thoughts
by living in the past among familial difficulties?

Three Faces

I am not so simple as to have a split personality like slices
of pie.
I am not a bite-full.
I am the taste that is indistinguishable from the snack.
I am the pumpkin.
I am the pie.
I am a forkful of my own taste without pecans,
nuts....
I am nuts you know.
Delicious to be mad and as incoherent as the hatter.
I am not a bite.
I am the whole pie.
I am not a forkful.
I am not insane.
I am a spoonful of confusion.
I am not the three faces of Eve.
I am the consistency of three personalities all touching
each other's being.
I can't tell me from me because I am at the bottom of
what I be,
a mouthful of myself in a batter of pumpkin taste.
I am not Joanne Woodward.
No, I did not win the Academy Award for acting.
I acted on trying to coordinate diverse personalities on their edges.
I blended.
I did not distinguish.
Transgenders are the simpleminded trying to be different
than their stasis,
people hiding from themselves because they are bored

with their genitals.

I am not the entrance to insanity.

I am just the crack when the door is left partially open.

Psychotic Me

I called myself psychotic because I wanted to be bigger than neurotic.
Insanity is large and being off and on is neither.
I want to be crazy so that the popcorn in my head pops
and the salt is missing with my judgment.
Ah, butter popcorn,
there's the rub.
I do not have hallucinations.
I am an hallucination.
I don't know me.
I am the impression that wanders into my meaning like a dunk
in a donut.
I am deluded.
Big deal.
Misjudgment is a failure to see straight when astigmatism is here
or there or everywhere in its failure to see what is and isn't
in the cataract night.
It is not that I am insane.
It is that I am somewhere on the border between madness and
cognition.
I am a little off the edge.
I am hanging from the cliff by a clump of grass like the time in
summer camp
in 1960 when I held onto my life by green weeds.
I am not abnormal.
I am your misperception of me going back to you.
I see double when I don't wear my glasses with their prisms.

Oz

I walked out of my mind and felt apples bouncing against my head thrown by fictional trees in the Wizard of Oz.

Dorothy was with me. She had been with me since I was twelve and I first fell in love with her singing, "Somewhere over the Rainbow."

I have never been in a mental institution. I have always been an outpatient, one of the mildly insane.

Now at seventy- three I feel my old child's heart beating for Dorothy again and again. She is a permanent totem pole. She is magic. I see her like I did the first time that I saw her and approached the Emerald City.

I was a man of many colors. Magic was in the air like I didn't care what was and what wasn't in rainbow fragility.

I let the classic movie slide down my back and enter rags of psychic fake probity. I am serious about living in a colorful land and it doesn't matter whether I am in or out of Oz.

It's only in madness that I feel sane and identify with the various pieces of my brain. I like the weirdness in me and accustom myself to the collision of scrabble pieces that spell nothing but confusion.

Shapes

I am the correspondence of similar pentagons in my disordered self.
I look like me.
I am the reflection of myself in the jerkwater tide of my magnificence.
Do you know me?
I don't.
But the engine of my brain churns out locomotion like a train
racing from Indians in the wild, wild west.
I am a thinking machine.
I am the wildlife running outside myself in the African plains.
My posture is hunched from the weight of the world but I am still
what I am which is life in an elephant's trunk,
in a pig skin wallet.
I'm not sure that you like me.
I'm not sure that I like me.
I am not sure that I am me or that the pheasant under glass is
already dead.
Love is a beacon.
I shine across the bay on myself and remember that I grew up in
Great Neck.
F. Scott Fitzgerald lived near my house and Gatsby looked out
from King's Point at the green light at the end of Daisy's dock.

Language Salad

Word salad tastes good when you spread French dressing on it
and speak in a foreign accent.

You chop up the lettuce and the pieces rankle like disorganized speech.

I am not hebephrenic. I am Caesar salad, a dictator over my
writing. I taste the taste of who I am.

I get pieces of green caught in my teeth and I can't separate my
thoughts and mind from the taste of my language.
Is cucumber part of my mental disorder or are the carrots the
cause of madness?

You think I speak nonsense but I am crunching out the delusion of poems.
I am a mad side course.

I make no sense but I make all the tasty salad sense in a world
where words are chopped green peppers or pieces of cucumber.
Call me hebephrenic.
I am almost coherent.
I don't care.

I just want to make a serving for a mess,
a salad for the future,
a bowl of accidental coherence in the salt and pepper.

It is not that I make sense but that the words keep flowing out of me like a tempting appetizer until the bowl is licked clean.

Cataracts

I am happy to talk to myself so that I don't have to let
a third party interfere
with my connection,
my erection bending into myself,
my glorious grandeur and heat near my nakedness.
I am so lucky to be me because I am someone I know
and get along with when the world falls apart
around me like mud from a horse's hooves.
I like the way I look at me and the surprise sadness
of feeling apart from myself
while still somewhat together in conversation.
I am so many personalities that all gather themselves
Into a crowd of psychotic tendencies
but I am not mean
I am the dream of someone else to master differences
and live on the other side of obfuscation.
I see myself clearly as if I had already had my cataracts out
which I will in two weeks
even if it doesn't matter
even if I will look myself in the eye and see the retina of truth.

I am Only Interested in Me

Most people are concerned with learning to know other people.
but I don't give a shit.
I am only interested in me and I am as narcissistic as a flower
or that Greek fellow who fell in a pool.
I am drowning in myself
like a breath caught in water
and I don't give a damn what you think of you or me.
Sometimes I am aroused by myself and dance naked in front
of the mirror and hold my dick with octopus arms.
If the world disappeared it wouldn't bother me because I am the
world and what goes on around me doesn't matter.
God has made me in his replication
and I am the holy ghost and the spirit and the son and whatever
else I be,
you see,
I am all that and then some as I plug my thumb up my ass so that
I block more of myself inside my digestion.

The Congestion of my Face

I am not who I am and am who I am not which comes down to a
lot of excessive
anxiety and the feeling that the nervousness won't stop.

My personality is split
like a abandoned
identity
in a boat yard where
the hulls have holes in them.

I have seen the congestion of my face and how it has broken
down into variable photos.

It's not that I am restless
but that I am little pieces
of consistency
broken down into irritable candies.

When I look in the mirror I know who I am and find that firmness
has tension beneath it and I can't sleep so good at night when I
am looking back at me.

Addiction

When I was young I had problems with impulse control disorders. I couldn't resist repetitive discord. At times I drank too much alcohol and snorted too much cocaine. I was a binge taker. I didn't go on and on for years in continuous highs. I did not whittle my health away with an addictive knife.

I flew high when I wasn't high. I didn't want to punish myself. I was already hurt. I lived with a broken wing. My pain was deep. I reveled in it.

After a few years of cocaine I started playing around with the idea of quitting. My mafia, three-hundred-pound dealer, showed up at my office on Sixth Avenue. I bought a couple of thousand dollars' worth. I then went to the office bathroom and flushed it down the toilet. I didn't even snort a line. I had to hurt myself to get whole. I became a world of moral redemption.

The next week I called my dealer back. I bought another thousand dollars' worth. I went to the toilet again and flushed it. I was cured by throwing it out. During the last thirty-five years I never touched cocaine again. I taught myself a lesson. I was a teacher writing abstinence in chalk on my forehead.

Quitting alcohol was easier. I went to jail for two years and I couldn't get any wine. One day a cellmate of mine sneaked in contraband vodka. I turned him down. I didn't want to get busted by the feds.

When I got out I had an occasional drink. It no longer appealed to me so I didn't have to worry about going cold turkey. My will-power was dominant like stone.

My addictions were minor. Now I was free. Addictive behavior is an extension of feeling sorry for yourself. I loved myself. I was manic. I was jubilant in my freedom from addiction. Confidence grew in me like a flower garden. I stung myself like a bee. I liked the pain. I doused myself in a sprinkler system of happiness.

My Dementia

I am between books so I don't feel like writing another poem.
What for?
I am between closure and hopscotch.
I don't want to begin again when I've just finished.
It's not that I am a poem but that I am the distillation
Of elevated language.
I am the answer to questions never asked
And the nonchalance of a failure to get serious.
So what that I don't exist.
I am my own namesake—David.
Throughout all the confusion I find a Yellow Brick Road
and follow Dorothy in my favorite movie to Oz.
It's magic.
I am a gadget.
I am the rigid toy of my own onset of dementia.

I Hate Myself

So I walk down the streets of Manhattan to rise into the feeling
that New York is cemented inside of me.

I am the buildings.
I am the traffic lights.
I am the stores.

I adore New York and myself even though I am seventy-two and
readying for death. I live on Seventy-second street. Isn't that a
kick in the ass? Cheek to cheek.

The horse paws the air as he waits for his next fare.
Fair enough.
Impatience for discomfort is a human
and animal trait.

I have lived. I have died. I have lied that I have been this or that
when I have rarely knocked the ball out of the park with a bat.

Pin a map on my back.
I am New York. I hate New York. I hate myself.
I don't even know what I mean when I mean what I don't know.

My neurologist says I'm a little demented. I am old. But I have
been confused since I was a child. There is noise in the air.
It rains pellets.
I get wet.
Due to my 1993 tax evasion I am in debt.

Where will it end? As if I didn't know. The only question is when will my eventual punishment be worse than what I feel day to day and when will the traffic light turn permanently red?

I Am It

If you were me you wouldn't always get along with yourself
because your moods would throw rocks at each other like stones skipping
across a lake.

I can't get along with myself.
I fight.
Then I kiss my hand and am in love
again
with who I am and who I am not.

I know myself a little and it doesn't really matter because they are
all just words without valences,
matters,
defining ideas that are blown in the wind.

I always feel that I am on the edge
of falling off a cliff
even though I know I wouldn't be
on a cliff
because I am afraid of heights.

Six Billion People

You have nothing to do with me because you and the rest
of the world don't exist
and I am what I am which is the jam, jelly
and spread on the bread of my soul, my being,
my extant existence.

Six billion people in the world and they are all inside of me.
I am the population of the diverse globe
and drain the multiple faces down to one man.
I am that man.
I am the world's arrogance.

I am very David in my own world.
I am not in Michael Jackson's world because I do not chase
children.

In this world I am looked down on for being straight.
The left wing has flown into insane prejudices.
They have reversed normal values.
They embrace the failure of opposites.

Difference is lauded by the different.
I am the lack of imagination in a failure to find perversion.
Diversity is the goal of the twisted, dimwitted seekers.

Genius

I think I am a genius and don't care that you don't recognize me
as something other,
something larger,
a day in the Alps near the snowfields where I lay down
a blanket
and go all the way with you like two little piggies.
I am not deluded.
I am the delusion that is hidden beneath the determination.
I am your night.
You are my day.
We pass twenty-four hours when I am not angry at you depending
on the vicissitudes of my moods.
You call me bipolar.
That is only a name or a label on a jar of Schmuckers.
I am the interstices among the diagnoses that the doctors pin on me
like a Band-Aid on my forehead.
But what if I am really a genius and everyone else in the world is
a dope.
I don't take dope.
I don't believe in obfuscation or obscuring the result
with the purple haze of rock
and roll medicines.
My generation ignored me and failed to recognize that I was the one.
I was even the two;
twice the one.
twice Jesus.
Not in his ability to spout clichés and hang from the cross
but in my having the whole world in my hands and throwing it
across the velvet table like a gambler at craps.

I never knew what I didn't know but I know it like I had lived through it yesterday.

My Prescription

You make me angry when you withdraw or attack or fail to notice
me dancing on the edge of a cliff with an umbrella over my head
to keep off the rain.

I am you.
You are me.
And sometimes self-hatred
separates us.

I am holding onto the back of a train as I run across the country
beneath the black birds that want to poke out my eyes.

At the height of my manic depression
I wanted to blind myself.
Not really
but I thought my hands would take control
and stab a pencil into my eyes.

It was its worst in jail. I was locked into my obsessions.

It's the thoughts that intrude that frighten you, which is me, with
things that I am afraid that I can't control even though I can as
long as my prescription for lithium is refilled.

Being David

I Am Very David

I told you I wanted to write a book about how I am a flawed character,
a chip off the old potter's block,
a cut in my hand.

You said you loved the idea and that I should call it, "Being David."
I don't know if I am David.
I might just be my middle name,
"Henry."
Yet somehow, I decided to name the book, "I Am Very David."
I be who I be and I am whomever I am.
I am very.
I am the man.

I come and go with no direction,
entering my exits and leaving the slot of my entrances.
I would hang myself
like my roommate, Billy, in Schuylkill Federal Prison Camp.
I didn't see him hanging because he did it
when he moved to Allenwood.
I would have liked to see him hanging because I am fond of the dramatic.

When they put me on roadwork I hoped that the CO's would whip me.
I wanted to be tough,
a manly poet,
a contradiction like I was when I boxed as a pro.

My next cellie, Eddie, overdosed on heroin the following year.
So many die.
I don't cry.

I like to say, "Well done, my friends."

The prison shrink thought I was crazy but didn't he notice that I lived longer than my room mates?

Death is crazy while life is the peach pit of sanity on the branch of learning.

Captain America

I am Captain America, living in my own fifty states of ultra-consciousness. I am not a superhero. I am not Chris Evans. I could probably take him in a fight. I was once almost as good-looking. I am seventy-two, skip to my loo. What you gonna do?

I enter the cities of my own despair, in love with whom I am and who I am not.
I have nothing to do with your country when I am surrounded by my geography.
I am a patriot. I am not. I have no wish to save my country.
Only myself.

I watch the President on television and am glad that I don't have to pick up his sticks. I don't like to play political games. I am a serious God. I am spiritual not practical.

Obama did curls with ten pounds. Embarrassing. A weak state of mind is reflected in a weak bicep.

I don't want to speak to millions of people and decide whether to raise the minimum wage, get involved with trade or make peace with the Taliban.

Save me from responsibilities other than to be true to introspection and find love in the mirror of my heart.

The President walks away from himself into the jungle of mundane decisions
and interactions with people he doesn't care to engage. He wears

the false face of the Joker. I am bored looking at him or the previous Presidents.

The President is torn apart by the demands of pedestrian morons. Americans are stupid. The politicians pretend that they are intelligent.

I am me. You are you. *Whip de doo*. It doesn't matter. Sometimes I feel like the mad hatter. We both don't matter either.

I am the captain of self-love following the heart rather than regulations. Don't hate me for this:

I am a spiritual atheist who finds God under my shoulder pads. I am not Colin Kaepernick. I do not chew on self-importance. I am a genius who feels like a dope. Colin is a real dope who boasts his absent genius. He fumbles the ball. I score a touchdown without playing the game.

Identity Politics

If you went my way would you end up looking like me in the lamplight or being me in the broad sun?

Would you swallow my learning like a diet soda or spit me out like a failed opportunity?

Consider that I am you
and then I am not
and you are me
but you only wish it.

It's not a notion of identity politics but a consideration of not knowing how to cope with my identity.

I am ideas banging against each other like marbles as I play the game of life in the schoolyard.

Nothing Wrong

There is nothing wrong with me but something is right with me in
that I am blue
or another color or a red face in a watery lagoon.

So it goes.
So it doesn't go.
I don't care what I might or might not do.
I can't tell the truth because this life is a lie.
I die.
I resurrect.
What the heck I am vaguely conscious of who I am.

I am glad that I ride this horse of a body until I come out the
opposite edges.
I love the fish in the pond and miss the riches that I buried be-
neath the shrubs.

I am here, there and everywhere.
And nowhere.
I wish I could make up my mind to confirm that I had a mind
instead of confusion
In the neighbors' back yard.

You call me crazy because you don't understand the intelligence
of a boiled brain
In a festival of eggs.

I guess I am who I am like ham which is not kosher but kosher is not ham and I prefer the pig.

I put on a wig to hide my bald spot. I am too old to hide from reasonableness and too young to actually be young when I am not.

Chunks

I am little chunks of mental wood in a plastic bag which I carry to
my home to pile into building blocks of intelligent madness.

I died.
I separated into squares
of madness.
I am the result of a conclusion
that never arrived.

Chop me up and let me battle against my sharp shapes so that I
cut the elbows of my brain into warring thoughts.

I am me.
You are you.
I don't give a damn what either
of us do
when we do or don't do it.

The personalities that live inside of me are not integral but are
capable of fusing in contradictory roles of integration.

My selves are busing from one neighborhood to another in order
to integrate my divergent psyches.

I am Boston in the sixties busing my divisive personalities into
cohesiveness. There is civil unrest in my frazzled brain.

Wide Disappearance

I don't know who I am but I know who I am not which is not your
impression of me or the label you stick on my forehead.

I put a stamp above my eyebrows
and send myself to China
to ignore the Chinese
and find distance in a short rope.

You call me a Jew but I am not so simplistic. I am David. That is
a ballistic religion that is as confused as North Korea.

I want to have nothing to do with you
if I can confirm that you are irrelevant
and a distant affirmation
of nothing.

There is no sense in defining myself when I am the absence of
ideation and the necessity of wide disappearance.

Understanding

I ran into this personality with the other direction in a confused rant.
I am not me.
I am not you.
I get upset when I fall onto my side.
I am whatever I do when I define myself by actions
that sneak past me like bars of soap in a communal bath.
You smell good.
I do too.
What's the difference?
It's not that many years until we die.

If I understood myself I would get along better with my imitation
of who I wanted to be.
But I escaped from myself at about six when I formed a Freudian
personality that didn't work as it should.
I was stuck in my root beginnings.

You tell me that I am difficult to get along with.
What do I know about communal jests?
I don't care if you have trouble with me.
I have trouble with me too.
I rub the edges of my personalities
and bleed.

It's not that I don't understand myself but that myself rebels
against my understanding and lives in the map that rolls itself
up and hides in disappearing countries.

Dissociative

Am I *The Three Faces of Eve* or the *Sixteen Faces of Sybil*? I have never seen either movie. I am a movie. How does a movie watch a movie? With my cataracts I am almost blind. Until I cut them out.

I can't afford the Lasik surgery. It is twenty-five hundred dollars per eye. Thirty years ago I bought a Rolls Royce like it was the price of a Volkswagen. I was rich. When I got out of jail I went to a diner. I skipped the French fries because they were too expensive—three dollars and fifty- cents.

Life goes up and down and then you're found skipping around your plot at the graveyard.

I am the thousand faces of David.
I am not staccato.
I am not a panel in a Japanese tea room.
I am an agreement of profiles.

I am the spider web without the spider that runs between this and that like a watery solid and a fair skin in the game.

I do not gel.
I am not the solid rock of cracked personalities.
I am not schizophrenic.
I am the float; I am the balloon.

I am the rubber raft torn to shreds in the knife waves of the ocean. But I am not multiple personalities. I am one giant squid

that wobbles around beneath the waves like I have the whole
world in my tentacles.

I am the nothing that is everything and find something in difference.
In my opposition I find an undercurrent of sameness that is comforting.

I am not dissociative.
I am the glue that binds the stretch of distance in the travels of madness.

I am not separate identities. My personalities are not distinct. I am
not split. I am fused. I am the merging of various clusters of
perception and memory.

I am not fragmented. I am melded into a collage of differences, a
blend of distinctions.

Reading my poems is watching a movie because I am framed by
the opening up of my personality in the theater of my self-display.
Eat some popcorn. Have a soda. Skip the beer. I threw up after
drinking thirteen bottles in 1964. Here's wishing you were as
complicated as me or a simple casket in a graveyard.

Neither This nor That

Confusion is something I don't know how to interpret because it is
by definition a rolling fog on a wet wave.

Fine?
Define?
I don't know anything but navigation.

I don't know this nor that
neither because I am becoming senile
nor because I was hit too much in the head when
I was the world's oldest boxer.

But I do prefer being out of it in a confused manner of not making
sense of anything at all.

I don't mind being almost mindless
but acuity is a fool's errand
to pick up groceries
and come back.

Let me be other than I am so that I am not the strident exigencies
of failed imagination in a nap.

Thread

Whenever I have a conversation with myself I listen to my ideas
and find them quite convincing.
I like you.
I like me.
I like what we say to each other when our lips aren't moving.
Everything that is internal starts in both the outside world
and in the inner tumult of cascading moods.
It's not that I am introspective but that I am inside out like
a glove pulled out of the snow and reversed so that it could dry.
I am an escape from the outside world
like a criminal who has run from the interior of a jail.
When I get to know myself fully I will have a love affair
with who I am and who I am not
like a surprise introduction to the thoughts that thread my mind.
A thimble of protection keeps me from the madness that sews me
together.

Sushi

I can't get along with myself so I hit myself in the head
and try to knock the distractions from me.
I hate me.
I love me.
I hate loving me and love hating me.
I am David.
I am Henry.
I am Lowenkron.
I am Lawrence.
Somewhere in the middle of all this language is reality.
If I bump into myself, I will bounce into some other ideas
and find the truth in a bruise.
I know you for who you are not.
You are not me.
But you are me when my eyes are closed and I can't see
the truth.
If only I liked me more than I disparaged my demeanor
by turning a cold shoulder against myself.
I am Frosty the Snowman.
I am struggling with the winter of myself in an isolated igloo.
I pull a fish out of a hole.
I cut fluke with a thin knife.
I eat it raw.
I find sushi in my frozen personality and the bill is reasonable
compared to nouveau riche Nobu in pretentious Tribeca.

Hello Me

I introduce myself to myself and find that I am not myself
but someone other than other
and wishing on a tree
to be the bark
and lifting my leg like a poodle to piss away
the years.
Time is what time is and going is coming when the rain
falls on the beauty of peonies.
I don't know what I don't know and knowing is the absence
of not knowing
in the presence of picking up all the sticks in the game.
You don't remember me because I have forgotten myself.
I am what I am not and am not what I am as I get lost
in other people's ideas and forget that it all doesn't matter.
I fell to earth to rise up like a rose and don't notice
London Bridge falling down behind me nor my fair lady
building it up with bricks and mortar.
But it will not stay like I will not stay because I can't find
the strut in my step or the step in my strut.
Who am I?
It's funny that I don't know who I am but recognize the terrorist
who crashes his van into innocent people on London Bridge.
To forgive a killer is to risk the life of a saint.
Vengeance is magnificent.
I like being frisked.
It grabs my self-importance.
I would stop and frisk God if He were acting strange and throw
Him with Bloomberg into the river to mock his moist apologies.

Lacking Religion

If I bumped into me would I know that I am me or would I
misinterpret the accidental assault on my indifference,
my isolation,
my conglomerate parts?

I am a broken-down blimp.
Do blimps break down?
No, they are too soft,
too canvas,
too not solid enough to piece into infinite slivers.

I have as many pieces of personalities as Ronald Regan had jelly
beans in his jar.
I thought he was a war monger.
But he stopped wars through might and tore down the wall,
ending Russia's long night.

I don't know me from another.
I am the cracks in an orchestra of a squeaky violin.
I am on edge.
I am the edge.
I jump like Hans Solo's leap over the cliff and am saved by faith.
I have no faith.
I am the atheist in the church who shows up out of curiosity just
to see if I believe in anything.
I don't.
But I respect the church goers and would never shoot them in Texas
even if I were a killer and had the urge for no reason to get back
at religion for trying to give me so much.

A Thousand Personalities

My bonnie is dead. She lies over the ocean and the sea.
You don't need to bring her back to me.
She is me.
I am not transgender.
I identify with all people because I am a face in a crowd.
I am not Scottish.
Although my alcoholic maternal grandfather's name was Malkin.
I am a piece of Malkin.
I am a part of a thousand personalities.
The part of me that I know doesn't know who I am.
I walk New York's streets to be a cog in the city.
I am a log where I cut myself down
and lay in a river.
I am everything that I am not and not solely the thing that I am.
I am cute.
Not any longer now that I am seventy-two.
But I was when I didn't realize it.
Girls liked me because they didn't know me.
I liked me for the same reason.
I was the answer to the question that was never asked and
invented the question mark to discover answers.

The Joke

I introduce myself to myself and find that I am a stranger.
I don't control my thoughts.
Ideas control me but they are not my ideas.
They are Gods?
That's a joke for you idiots who believe in something outside
of yourselves where existence makes believe
and the spirit borrows a body.
I am me.
I am we.
I am all this and all that in a 57 Chevy turning time on its wheels.
Remember Sal Mineo.
Remember James Dean.
I am the coolness of an ice cube evaporating on a hot plate.
The fifties were a sweet ride.
They stank.
A bunch of dumb gangsters in the rumble seats of their lives.
I am beautiful.
I am the heart of the heart and the soul of the soul in love
with my hand when I have a grip.
If I ever get to know me I will abandon me because I can't get
along with the homunculus inside of the façade.

The Son

Daisy Duke doesn't raise her dukes to beat a young actor' nose.
She puts a shawl over her face and turns
from the action,
gets traction in her own solitary cashmere threads.

Her prettiness is lonely because it gets used by horn dogs who sniff
at Daisy's skirts and feel her up where they can.

I don't really know who Daisy is, you know,
I never saw the television show.

I don't watch white trash gesticulating nor do I hang with black
homeboys.

I only like myself. You don't have to forgive me for solipsism when
you don't even know what it means and are distant
from my introspective pose.

Daisy Duke? I don't even know the other characters in the show.
I don't care.
Popular culture is not popular with me.
I am air escaping from a lung and breathing back into itself
like life.

I am me. I am not me. I am life.
I am the Son of God but I am not arrogant enough to create a ruckus
like Jesus did.

Words

Wordy is its own definition and the truth lies within the spelling like a façade finds itself on the outside of the interior.

I want to write about nothing because the emptiness of the jar of meaning is the mother of invention.

Out of space comes satellites.
If we shoot off towards Mars
Mars comes to us.

I want to pull the rabbit
out of its lettuce bed of words
out of the hat of betrayal.

Let the words rub elbows with their syllables and language be its own delight like an Ice Cream Sunday.

The verbs don't mean.
They deem sounds like yoke inside of eggshells.

It's not in the saying that direction becomes determinant but it is in the pronouncing that we find self-generating walks in enchanted forests where magic is fundamental and trees are the absence of outside light.

I Don't Understand

I don't know what I mean and I don't care if I mean anything or
nothing or something that I don't understand.

I have separated from myself
like a minnow
let out in the ocean to swim
to reconciliation
with its death.

Who am I?
I am the disappearance of a pretty good lifetime into a calm
extraction of my tooth from food.
I am David.
Different from the other millions sharing my name.

And when I am gone
I will be gone
with the wind like Clark Gable
like Vivien Leigh
like the cyclical death of all the people
in the world.

But it is not only death because it is the words dripping from the
blackboard meaning nothing
to the chalk.

So much means nothing to me that I find comfort in giving up the
language that confused me.

Therapy

When I ran into myself I ran from myself because I was afraid of whom I would find in the creases of my brain where I hid from myself like a prisoner from his cellmate. Not that I ran from mine. I liked all three of my sequential cellies. I am linen. I am folded. I can't see what I can't see because I don't want to see who I am and who I am not.

You don't recognize me because you are me. You are too close to get a perspective. It's like you are wearing binoculars and your eyes turn into themselves. Like my cataracts. I am old. My sight is impaired. I am having an operation next week. I will see what I can see again.

I spent years in therapy and found confusion like a minnow in a pond. I hooked my psychiatrists with a jovial thread and I believe that I was entertaining. I liked that they liked me and found truth in their comments.

I admired their admiration because I felt that they could appreci-ate my genius. I am literary. I am not a genius in math. Numbers make me stupid. I am not an engineer. I am words on the page. I am not a politician. I do not lie to myself.

I do not make mundane decisions. I do not decide about train schedules or food stamps. I am a poem.

It's on the nose to say that I am all categories of mental illness. Not that I am sick. I dabble at the fringes over craziness but never end up trapped in the curtains between the acts.

Your opinion of my genius is stupid. I believe what I believe and I am what I am whatever that is. Call me what you like. I am not this or that.

It was fun seeing my shrink today. Actually, I didn't really see him. We both saw me. I was the target at the archery range at Birchwood Summer Camp in 1959.

My life keeps coming back to me like regurgitated concentration. I am the arrow I shot and the boomerang I threw when I was twelve.

Self-definition

I am not David because I am someone buried beneath the name
of David and I live in a hole, manifesting myself in disappearance.

I come.
I go.
I am two stars in the eye of a ho who wants
to be famous.
But I am not Stormy Daniels.
I am not Michael Avanti.

How can I define me? I can't find the meaning beneath my
evaporated personality.
I don't know who I am or where I've gone.

I died in another life.
It wasn't me.
I disappear like memories.
I am not not and am the distance that mountaineers climb.

What can I say about myself that isn't said by the way I walk into
a room or sit in a chair or just happen to be whomever I be.

Paul said, "Let it be." I am me. I be. I am what I am. I am a
narcissistic man. I am proud of it. If you find me self-centered,
get out of my center.

I am blind. I look into myself and am defined.

The Silent Spring of Eternal Confusion

I am startled by meeting me in the silent spring of eternal confu-
sion. Are these flowers in my hair or burrs cutting into my scalp?

I have run the gamut like Jesus
running with his cross
across self-destruction and
love of death.

So you say who I am and you don't know because you are not me
and don't reside in my head with all the neurotic filaments like a
lightbulb of shining pain.

It doesn't matter what I do because
I am a package on a conveyor belt
on my way to the end
of failure.

I am this or that because it doesn't really matter when I smack
my head against the wall and try to beat the sense out of my sadness.

Aging like Woody

Sometimes I wake up and I get scared that I don't know where I am. I see my desk and chair but I don't know what they mean and if they are part of my room or imported from another bedroom in a different dimension.

Is my mind from outer space? Am I a foreigner in an alien brain? Am I green and craggy?

I don't know where I am when I am where I am and I'm worried that I already died and am buried in my house along with the ghosts of my relatives. So many aunts and uncles dead. My parents fell from my life in caskets.

Sometimes I live outside of my body and look in at myself and say that I don't recognize the person that is me inhabiting my skin like a chipmunk in a tree hole.

My neurologist says I have dementia from being seventy-two and boxing for thirty-seven years. Did you know that I fought in Vegas and Atlantic City? I am proud of that. I wasn't that good. I was nuts. Squirrels picked me up in their mouths. I am their acorn. I am an unconscious shell.

There are times when I don't know if my thoughts are my own or if they are borrowed from a memory bank in the vast funeral of the sky.

When I am depressed I don't know if it is real or if I am making a big deal out of failed happiness and trying to enter a horserace of sadness. Am I trying to hurt myself as expiation?

I do not know why I am competing in depression like it is a blue
ribbon or a prize rather than falling from mania into the unfortu-
nate face of confusion.

I am the only man who has spent more years in psychotherapy
than Woody Allen when I had nothing wrong with me unlike
Woody who married his make-believe daughter and fucked up his
personal world beyond his sense of humor. And his child Dylan?
Who knows? The accusation is a condemnation.

I am old. My trousers are cold. I don't know if they are rolled. I
don't look around. I no longer have the fire or the desire. Peace
be with me, old man. I am Prufrock's cousin.

"Let us go then, you and I." Go where? Go how? I am the
"patient spread out against the sky." I have already gone into the
"restless nights."

I don't talk of Michelangelo. I am a crumbling statue. I am
David. I am a mind falling apart with surprise clarity. I know what
I don't know and don't know what I know.

Don't try to follow me. I am the maze that leads into its own
shrubbed interior.

It was Accidental

I disappeared from myself and left my glove in the other hand,
slapping myself with leather, not noticing whether or not I hurt myself.

I didn't mean to be me. It was accidental, fortuitous, an injury to
healthy diffusion where my life is poured into numbered glasses.

Am I bits of chemical in a vial or am I just vile in my refusal to be
the me that I be?
How can I be what I don't recognize and find identity in absence?

So time goes by and I go by as difference in fraternity and a
failure to understand who I am not and who I am.

I am a reflex action like a knee jerk when a doctor hits it with a
hammer. I am neither here nor there but I don't really care
because nothing matters when the matter Is beaten from me by
my own mistaken analysis.

I live in the generation of self-identity. But everyone identifies
with groups, nations, religions and colors instead of themselves.

I love Martin Luther King for letting me discover that the content
of your character matters more than the color of your skin. As if
I didn't know that.

Skin deep is thin and brainless whether from the left or the right.
Love is the colorless human heart.

The End

I don't give a damn if the world goes hot or cold or is blown up in
a nuclear explosion where pain goes numb in its grandeur.

I don't care if I eat sugar
or fats
or rat poison
because what the heck?
The heck takes
the gumption out of me.

I am chicken gumbo in the cold soup of the world.

So what if mothers worry about the fate of the planet as if it
matters when we are all dying a little bit each day.

I don't care particularly if I die because
I won't know the difference
when the lights go out
and I scuba dive into the Titanic wreckage.

What difference does it make if I am gone when the world has
only a few thousand years left?

I am more worried about nuclear weapons than some silly global
warming.

Memory is my maintenance if I manage to make it into the circus of the great literati with all the beauties fallen from the trapeze, onto their faces.

In the end is my beginning and the weight of sorrow is the happenstance of tomorrow.

Seeking my Self

Self-hurt

The order in my disorder is my desire to hurt myself whether mentally or physically. I feel closer to myself when I am wounded. There is love in sadness. As a teenager I cut myself with razor blades (lightly), punched myself in the face and broke my hand on the concrete driveway wall in our mansion in Great Neck Estates.

F. Scott Fitzgerald lived in the Estates. He wrote better than me. He hurt himself by drinking too much. That's a coward's way out. I'm no coward. I don't sip on the teat of whiskey. Although in my thirties I drank about ten drinks a day and snorted thick lines of coke. I didn't take it seriously. I was just playing. I didn't fall off the seesaw in the playground.

I like to get hit bluntly. When I was a boxer I dropped my hands so tough Hispanic opponents could hit me in the face. That made me feel closer to them. You hurt me, I hurt you. It was like my relationships with women.

The times I got knocked out were like orgasms. I tingled. I went numb. I disappeared into unconscious pleasure.

In Denver they had to wake me up with smelling salts. There is something about being knocked out that is like the numbness of sex.

I once stood next to a neighbor's huge tree and scraped my cheek against the bark. It was Floyd Patterson's house. He bought his property from my dad. I scraped myself against the bark of a tree. The blood dribbled. I could have done better. I could have been a big accident rather than a scrape.

When Floyd was punch drunk he was the boxing commissioner. He didn't remember that he had been my neighbor.

I was driving my dad's Lincoln before I had a driver's license. I was in the back roads of King's Point. I was worried about getting drafted for Vietnam. I thought it was better to die now. I held the steering wheel with my hands and slid my head down on the seat. I was hoping to crash into a tree.

But the self-preservative, self-curative part of me raised my head back up so I could see the road and avoid crashing. I wanted to die. I wanted to live. I never really knew what I wanted because my desires were independent of me and I led several lives in contradistinction to their leanings.

I guess I have always been driving on the back roads of King's Point trying to decide whether to crash into a gate or a tree.

Everest

I identify with your identity because I am nothing more or less
than what I am not,
not this,
not that,
not a figment of your or my imagination.

When I climbed Mt. Everest I realized that I was in my bed
imagining I was a Sherpa skipping across ladders
and crevasses.

I don't go anywhere much.
I am afraid of people and distant experiences on the other side
of snowy death.

I am not who I am but I will soon be the image of death and zero
will be printed on my forehead
like a stalactite piercing what's left of my frightened brain.

My fingers will fall off and I will grab my rope with my knuckles.
I will slip, slide and fall away.

When I am brain dead I will be better able to relate to activists.
There is nothing I hate more than idiots who feel their emotions
are honorable precipices that rise above others' feelings.

The Sense of Cents

I am juggling all my thoughts and listening to words knock into
each other like they meant something other than sound.

I am the stupid noise in a brilliant vase.
I am the light on the post
that I send
into the intelligence of my consciousness.

I don't think.
I am thought.
I am what I say even though there is no intention
In my vocalization.

I am a big chunk of the universe's consciousness in a planetary
lack of awareness of who I really am.

I am dead beneath the knowledge of who I am as a kind of
feeling but not a total ratiocination.

I am so involved with me that I can't see what is out there or
what is inside me.
Nothing makes sense.

Two weeks ago, I made no sense when I threw two hundred
pennies down the drain to prove that cents didn't matter.

Sick Thoughts

Sometimes I want to kill little children who pass me by with their mothers or their maids on the Upper East Side.

I don't really.
I am playing a game with my dark side.
I am death's dominion.
I kill.
I don't.
I am intrusive.
That's what my psychiatrist calls me.

I want to rape a young girl.
I lie.
I look myself in the eye and recognize that I want to hurt myself with thoughts that aren't mine.

I never hurt a child.
I never would.
But the thought that I would hurts me and brings me back to when I was a child and my mother punished me.

I like to hurt myself.
It is a game.
I am not insane; I am just playing with myself like a crooked smile.

Of Many Minds

When I walk past kids in baby carriages I want to take them out
and smash their heads on the ground. I want to rape their maids.
I want to poke out my eyes.

Twenty years ago in jail I used to sit on my hands at my tiny desk
so that I wouldn't shove my pencil into my eyes. About this
thought, I shiver. I quiver. I chime. I wonder how much time I
have left.

Oh, what fun in the city. I am witty and bright and a product of evil
thoughts. I am a killer who doesn't have the courage or desire to kill.

Actually, I am nothing. My thoughts don't even relate to me.
They are injections into my head from the great needle of cruel
ideas. A devil of a God infects me with the illusion that I am other
than I am.

I am hatred. I am bad. I am self-destruction without a bomb. I
splinter. I am fragments of a total personality. I am pieces of myself.

Sometimes I am scared of whom I am and then I realize that I am
not. I am a crowd of people of different temperaments at Times
Square at New Years. I am celebrating that I am a tourist in my own life.

But if I spent six hours in midtown in a crowd, how would I go to
the bathroom. I am scared of springing a leak. I would kill myself
before pissing in my pants.

Am I the confetti before the dropping ball? A product of what other people throw into the air to celebrate nothing for the sake of celebration.

Am I a joke? A funeral procession? It doesn't matter as long as I go on being whatever I am, doing whatever I do, sipping up life with a soup spoon.

Locked Up

I do not know if I am the evidence that a crime has been committed in that my mind is a hurt thing and the thing that is hurt is me.

I don't think straight
or flush
or play a full house
at cards.

Whatever I am I am not the answer to the question that disappears and the anxious disorder of self-hatred.

I don't know what I mean
when I mean less
than more
and confusion in a bouquet of petals.

I should be locked up with myself so that I can socialize with my various personalities and find hurt in self-analysis.

I Am a Mess

I can't think straight anymore or anywhere.
I can't think crooked.

I am a result of manic depression,
Obsession compulsion
and slow brain waves from boxing.

In my insane can of worms I feel free.

I am a wave that breaks on driftwood;
I am the salt water inside of a dune.

I don't know if I am going forward or backwards.
I don't know if I am stepping
on the joyous balls of my feet
or the heels of my depression.

I am a mess.
I am congealed into the sloppiness of false answers
In a seashore without questions.

The Water Gun

I shot myself in the head with a water gun so that I could approximate what it was to die.

Soggy story.
No bloodshed glory.
There was no trauma or drama.

Death by water would be drowning in my backyard on Lake Montauk before my family went the way of all flesh.

Who stole my gun?
I want to shoot the afternoon clouds
and find death lonely.

Should I add some shampoo to my bald spot and give life to disappearing hair in the air in the bare reality of aging.

Brain Matters

If I turn my brain inside out I won't know where is what.

The curlicues of gray matter don't matter
as much as the delicate neurons that spread across
my toasty ideas like peanut butter,
lacking jelly.

I don't know who I am.
I don't know who you are.
But I know who I am not and your absence from the school yard.

Confusion is avoidance and avoidance leads to dark disarray.
Is dementia preparation for death and do I have absence
to look forward to in a pool of nothingness
and a spray from a garden hose?

Nice to know me before I become you or your memory in my death.
If I look over my shoulder I see my blades twitching to music.

A Wooded Guy

I recognize myself as someone other than who I am and an
introduction to a space alien in the enchanted woods.

What do I know about me
when the leaves fall?
Am I a bare barking imitation of a dog
or a naked affront to normal
men?

I come back to myself on a forest path and kill Hansel and Gretel.
At least I fantasize that I am the cause of their deaths.

But I am gentle.
I am mild.
I don't kill anyone.
Don't accuse me of what you would like to do
in the raw bowels of your killer mind.

I am a monk.
I am a priest.
I am the spirit of peace and a piece of the spirit.

Don't call me a murderer or I will murder you in the jungle of my
twisted love.
I am peace.

I am a piece of a tangerine.

I am the sweetness that is tart to the tongue and dangerous to the escape.

My Wife is my Wife is my Wife

Adele's Voice

I am in the dentist's office. A painful place. But the music is a bird flying in the mountains. It is beauty staring into its own face as it flies over a lake. At first I don't know the song or the singer. But magnificence has its own definition and I later look it up on my computer and it is Adele singing "Someone like You."

Lauren, my wife, you are someone like you. You are more than less and meaning in opposition to similarity. I love you accompanied by this sad song which has nothing to do with the beauty of our relationship. We come together. We never go apart. We are polarities coming together from different ends of the globe.

"Someone Like You" is about breaking up. We've been a couple for fifty years and will die together. We will walk up the mountains until we fall off a cliff into each other's arms.

Adele sings, "Never mind, I'll find someone like you/ I wish nothing but the best for you, too." And she accepts love's death like I sprinkle its plant life with a watering can. I celebrate the best for us two. We are one. We are everything in a mountain range.

The beauty of you is that I will never find someone as ethereal as you. You are the light that shines through a cloud.

Adele sings, "Sometimes it lasts in love, but sometimes it hurts instead."

For me it hurts in lasting because love is so beautiful that it is as painful as Adele's voice making me think of you and the experi-

ences we've been through. We are all the king's glory. We are
the queen's jewels.

You are the beauty of Adele's voice. I look at you and want to
sing but I'm off key and we all have different beautiful attributes.
I do not need to be vocal. I listen to you like knowledge. You are
the guide to my internal encyclopedia.

Four O'clock Lunch

I am dining with my wife and myself at St. Ambrose.
I once sat next to Paul McCartney there.
He is not me.
He is a star.
I am a broken piece of a planet that is revolving around
like a chip off my old block.
It is not crowded here but there are people near us.
I hate crowds.
Even small approximate crowds.
After about an hour I tell my wife I want to leave.
She is playing with her I-phone.
I don't have one because I couldn't figure out how to work it.
Twenty more minutes pass until I can convince her to go.
She says she wants to stop at Ralph Lauren for a muffin.
All my organs shift angrily inside because I don't want
to sit in another restaurant.
I feel that I am going crazy.
I would rather hang myself than be a hanger out.
I do not want to be near people who are so very much people
that they infuriate me.
Keep me insulated from the populace.
I want to hide in myself like a kidney and keep away
from human touch.
I don't mean to be rude to my wife who likes to mix and match
with strangers.
It's only in loneliness that I discover I am and am not.
I am what I am which is the aggravation of stones inside me.

Jesse

I called my pharmacologist, Jesse, to get my blood test results. He said my lithium was .7 and my prostrate was 2.2. My lithium was usually .6.

"Is my increased level OK?" I asked. Perhaps, I needed more. I wanted to make sure that the madness was balancing on the bongo board of life.

"You just told me that you love your wife, you are writing creatively and you enjoy teaching boxing. You seem more than alright to me," Jesse said.

I guess I'm alright. At seventy-two I've found ways to be happy like throwing gliders in delicate winds. I float. I am balsa wood. I am what I am. I am David, man. I am manic. I am spare.

I rise up into the air like a model plane of my youth. The only thing I look forward to is dying with my wife. I want to hold hands with her as we walk across the threshold into some other place.

We will be beyond and then some. We will be present in outer space. We will invent heaven for our permanent picking of apples. Devil may care. I do. I am and I am not. I was once a snake. Now I am the curl of compromise.

Casino

I shuffle out the cards of my personality onto the gaming table and
I know that I am in love with the pictures and the high-powered scenes.

"Love me do"
as the Beatles sang
and I do love you,

the you that isn't you and the you that is you and all the you's that
are u-turns into themselves like I turn back into me.

There are high stakes in learning
the deck
and finding out which cards trump
and which slump
into loss.

I am the high stakes at the casino and I am all there is to the
game which is passing time and dollars in a diversion from the
self-embrace which involves my exposure.

I peek at your cards and see only hearts. I don't know what you
are thinking. We are gambling without emotions.

Enchanted

I found you on the other side of the river and you were me and
I couldn't tell the difference between what I was doing
and what I was saying
even though they were not cousins,
relatives
or similar in intent.

I don't know who I am and who I am not but the difference
is the same and not appropriate to the lack of reason.

You tell me that you know me
by my face
but that is merely the superficial
part of the blow in a fish's mouth,
the air that pushes out meaningless words,
not the lifetime we have been together.

Call me what you want and endeavor to know me as a painting.
I am a Van Gogh.

I never sold a lot of books in my lifetime but I lasted through the
centuries as the greatest unknown poet
who never cut off his ear but punched himself in the face
to feel life's fists somewhere between love,
hate and the confusion of familiarity.

Emily Dickenson and Herman Melville also knew what it
was to be lost in the woods when the trees wouldn't notice
them and they were kept going by the enchanted
apples thrown at us.

The trees are fighting with my future which is dragged into other people's pasts.

You are both my beginning and my end.

What We Mean

Sometimes I twist my thoughts up like twine. I am cat's paws
picking at myself. I am what sticks to the confusion and what
frays like wool. I am your everlasting love in a fork on the road
where we were supposed to go straight through to sanity. But we
are insane. We are not. If I just give up we will have a picnic
lunch beneath the trees and throw lilies on the pond. I love you as
much as I hate myself. If you pass the wine I will break the
bottle on my head and show you that I am willing to bleed for you.
Like you should care? What doesn't matter makes a big differ-
ence and I find I would marry you over and over like two spools
rolling down a hill in summer's diversion. I don't mean anything
that I say. I am its product. I am its meaning wrapped up as a gift.

Love Story

I am not looking at you now. You are still asleep at ten o'clock in the morning. Dream on, lover. Whether or not you are awake makes no difference. I have a very special relationship to the next room in our apartment where you are sleeping.

We don't sleep in the same rooms. There's something cool about that—a closeness and a distance. I touch you while our hands are separated by the door.

I don't know you. I know you. What's the difference when we have signed a document that we will stay together until we die? No one takes that seriously anymore. And yet our consistency is our sustenance.

I love you even though I don't have a clue who you are. You are representative of the fantasies that well up from inside me like a bucket being wound up from a stone well.

It doesn't matter if you are distant or cruel because distance is just a length to be shortened and cruel is a fear of intimacy.

I don't know if you are more intelligent than me or less. It doesn't matter as long as we orbit around the same interests in each other.

When I first met you you were young. I wondered how I would ever love the same woman forever. It seemed arbitrary. But love has nothing to do with your wife. It is a desire to be permanently attracted to the same magnet. It is the constant pull and pull of your anatomy.

As a young man I was as wild as bipolarity. I couldn't grab onto permanency. But here I am decades later anxious to get home from work to see you.

You were once the reason I wanted to travel. You are now the reason I want to be a sconce in the living room lighting your profile while you are writing a poem. I hope it is about me. Not that it matters. I have taken on the responsibility to be the chronicler of a great love story.

Fairy Tale Wife

I am mad as a hatter and protective of my head like a hat. I don't want to be in Alice's Wonderland but to share the rest of my life with my wife.

Who is she? Who am I? I am diffident about differences and remain undefined.

When I die my wife will die and we will ride through eternity in a Cadillac like Mel Brooks in *Blazing Saddles.*

We will shoot each other in the hands so that we don't die fast and don't feel bullets in our brains or dead bats in our belfries.

You are made for me and I am made for you but we don't discover who we are because we are too busy hiding from Indians.

Permanence is the words that fall from our tongues and we are statues in the desert like the pissing boy in Belgium.

We have been together fifty years and I remember a little or a lot because time is a gathering of emotions in a ranch.

I hang you from a lasso so that I can see your beauty suffocate. I then bang my head against a rock so that I can bleed out like a soldier in your brigade.

So many divorces in the world and we just keep getting closer. I know what it is to be part of your parade and to march with glory in a joyful route.

There were times we didn't like each other and times when love was in the air like an audience rooting for its home team.

I would rather die than to leave you because I could not gather myself together if you took my breath away.

I don't know who I am but you complete me so that I am my missing parts and other hints at total love and forever smooching.

Crazy as a Loon

When you go crazy it's because you are lazy about defining the
lines that are drawn in your head.
You don't want to see that the real thread is real
and refuse to draw in the logic with your fishing reel
because it is so much easier to be insane
and excuse your bad behavior and confusion with a name.
I am you and you are me and the proportion of neighborliness
is the happenstance of cohesion.
Name me insane.
Name me schizophrenic, or psychotic or the twist in the color blue.
I know I can bring myself back to academic brilliance and intelligence
like the twist in a bagel.
But I want to be the irrationalism in a mad cloud and piss rain
over the cattle who are reading books
and smoking pipes.
I am crazy as a loon while you see me as a lunatic, a goony bird.
I love you.
I love me.
And when I kill myself it will be an embrace with death.
Or it won't be.
I don't care.
When you take off your dress I get frilly and dizzy.
There is magic in the normal and terrific in the mundane.
I just want to be David in Wonderland with a hat on my head that
is magic in its madness.

9 789388 319584